How To Make Money.

STEVEN SCHOOL.

ISBN:1482611503
ISBN-13:9781482611502

DEDICATION

I Dedicate this book to those who simply wish to know where to begin on the road to building wealth.

CONTENTS

ACKNOWLEDGMENTS

I would like to acknowledge the folks at amazon for provide a way for ordinary people to publish their books and share knowledge with the world.

Let us begin our journey.

1 INTRODUCTION.

Hello there, and thank you for having the courage to get up off of that couch and do something about your financial future. I myself always dreamed of becoming wealthy, but it was difficult to know where to start, I racked my brain for a few years on this subject, at first it seemed like nothing would come to mind. I did not give up, I did not quit, and suddenly the ideas just began pouring in. I now have begun several ventures which build money. First of all, is knowing where to start, it only takes a little desire and willpower to get started. Let us begin to train our mind to think like the rich man, which is a good starting point. We need to evaluate everything in our life which costs us money and eliminate any of these subjects that we do not need, now is the time for wealth. Dating is expensive, put that aside for now. Cut frivolous spending on unneeded toys, evenings at the bar, whatever it may be because for the next twelve months we need to devote our free time to this plan, we can play later. I want you to plan a budget, it is very simple, always spend less than you earn, every paycheck we are going to save a little money, I don't care if it is only twenty five dollars a week at first. Cut frivolous spending, spend less than you earn, start saving money so that you can begin building up a little nest egg and have something to work with. Once this is permanently ingrained in our head, we can then move on to developing several different types of income, so that we have money coming in from many sources. If you are buying, buy low, if you are selling, sell high, always haggle for the best deal in situations where you can, it is the American way. You might consider at first, getting an additional part time job to expedite getting the financial ball rolling.

SAVINGS WITH INTEREST.

Now that we are off to a good start let us begin to save money, and to put that money to work for us. You can examine different banks online to determine what savings plans are available, and what the current interest rates are.

It does not hurt to have more than one account, let us not keep all of our eggs in one basket. I like to maintain an interest bearing savings account at my local bank, which is attached to my free checking account. I have also opened savings accounts at three other banks, and one online bank which is one of my favorites, Discover bank online. My wise and wealthy grandfather tuned me in to discover, you can set up this account online, attach it to your checking account, and transfer funds right from your home computer.

Now you know what to do with your tax return every year, I like to transfer mine straight to Discover bank. One key point to look for in a savings account, is that it is free, second that it bears interest, and third that it is FDIC insured. I personally do not lock my money down for ten year periods, I tend to go with money market accounts so that I have access to my funds, while showing an increase at the same time.

Now that we have determined several ways to begin saving our money, putting it to work for us, slowly growing and increasing those amounts over time, we need to examine several options to generate additional funds to feed those accounts, growing them into large enough quantities, that the interest becomes a sizeable amount as we are planning ahead so that years from now we can retire someday, and the sooner the better.

I personally believe that by retirement age, we need to not only have a sizeable nest egg, but that we need to have at least fifty five hundred dollars per month coming in, without even having to get out of bed.

During the course of this book we will cover several ideas to help get us closer to the goal, I am sure that you probably can come up with some additional ideas on your own to get you even further. Face it, in this day and age it is money which makes the world go round, it is the key to stability, security, and freedom. In most cases no one is simply going to just hand it over to us, if you want it, you have to make it happen yourself. One key principle secret of the rich, is that they spend less than they earn.

401K.

In these times, most companies offer a 401K plan, many of them will offer a partial matching system where they will contribute a certain portion of funds each time you make a contribution, up to a certain portion of your gross pretax income. It is important to enroll in your 401K plan as soon as possible.

I generally will either contribute the highest percentage of my income that my current employer will match, up to ten percent. If they are going to give us free money, let us take full advantage of it.

I like to choose my vestment options in the conservative areas, if you can get two percent interest with no risk of loss, this is ideal.

My 401K advisor balked at me, telling me that since I was still in my thirties I should go with an aggressive mix portfolio of investments, now I have known people who did this and who also lost thousands of dollars which crippled their retirement fund, he advised me that my choices would only net me a minimal two percent interest and that this at the time was equivalent to a savings account.

I politely informed him that I was happy to accept this secure rate of return, along with the fifty cents per dollar matching that my employer was also depositing into my account.

Six percent of my gross pretax income was going into this account, along with a free fifty cents per dollar, and two percent interest on top of the whole amount, with no risk of loss. In my opinion this is a good investment.

Some people theorize that if you want to win big you have to bet big, this is not always true, because it leaves you open to big irrecoverable losses. Let us remain conservative, and branch out into having several different incomes, money coming in from several sources, all being invested wisely, and conservatively. We must also always be on the lookout to eliminate anything which causes us to lose money. If we are going to generate business, let us first look to the options which are either free, or cheap, before we go and spend a large sum to journey into a venture which may fail. We need to cut expenditures, and maximize our profit margins.

START A BUSINESS.

I myself have started a few businesses, I have also been included in forming business ventures with partners. I maintain a full time job with 401K plan so that whatever happens, I have a weekly and steady check coming in while contributing to my retirement fund at the same time.

I will discuss some of these things with you, so that you may embark on whichever profitable options might suit you. I will show you how to abbreviate some of the options so that you can have a fast startup, with minimized investment. After all, the goal of business is to make money, not spend it.

All of the situations I shall present to you, are things that I have done myself.

I have for years, dreamed of writings books, and becoming a published author. However I never had the foggiest idea how to even begin, until one day I discovered on amazon, that they had designed just such a service, that I may write books, and that they will publish, advertise, print and deliver these books. There are two options, do it yourself for free, or choose the expert assistance option which is costly. Of course I spent the time to learn some of the techniques myself, so that I can utilize the free option.

It therefore does not cost me anything to publish a book, other than the electricity required to operate my computer. My goal in this endeavor is to write one hundred books, however long it takes me, in order to generate a residual lifelong retirement income. There are many subjects that I find interesting, and or have direct knowledge and experience with. Therefore I have plenty of subjects to write about, most of my books are self help guides designed for those who wish to learn in matters that I tend to be knowledgeable in. if you choose to follow this example, you can use the internet as a research tool to help you with whatever topic you choose. This truly is a great option since it is free and can lead to residual incoming funds that you can then transfer into your interest bearing savings account, thereby generating even more money. I believe that if you choose a wide array of subjects and topics to write about, there is a much higher chance of success, since you are catering to a wider audience. This is a simple thing that you can do in your spare time at home. Someone in a foreign country may be purchasing your books online even while you are sleeping.

IDEAS AND OPTIONS.

In the following pages we will delve into a few ideas to start a business, or generate cash, all of these I have actually done myself. And I can also verify, by my own personal experiences, that all of these things worked out well for me. We have already covered the portion of becoming an author and writings books in our spare time which is my personal favorite, I can write a new book while employees are out working and generating cash.

When I was younger I had wanted to begin a business breeding Bengal cats, I had friends and relatives who had experience with Bengals, Persians, and Abyssinians. The Bengal house cat is a hybrid breed between a Bengal leopard and a cat, giving you a little lap leopard. Many people have had great success selling these animals, I tried it only to discover that I am not really a cat person, but that I love the Rottweiler instead.

After selling my inventory of cats to another breeder, I purchased two German rotties from separate breeders. One female, and one male. These animals make wonderful pets and they are very protective of their owners. I was camping in the mountains of northern California in the summer of 2007, a bear came into my camp, my dogs charged at the creature and drove it away, ever since then a Rottweiler has always been the pet for me.

At close to age two, my dogs produced their first litter, one dozen beautiful puppies. At six weeks of age I placed a free advertisement online for them, which did not cost me a penny. Over the next two weeks all of the puppies were sold, I actually had close to two dozen people still wanting to buy dogs after they were all gone.

People were actually driving from other states to purchase these animals. The first litter alone put me well into the profit margin. What a great residual income indeed for something I can do in my spare time during my days off from work.

These dogs also patrol my yard and provide security, peace of mind knowing that my property is safe and secure.

In the past I had gone to work for a plumbing company that offered a ninety day training program, this company was a nationwide drain cleaning business, otherwise known as a rooter service. The training program was excellent, they also offered full service residential and commercial plumbing. After a little research I concluded that if one were to open such a business themselves, and if it only offered the rooter portion of the work where the highest profit margin seemed to be found anyway, that it could be done with a business license and liability insurance, since augering or snaking a drain does not in many cases require a master plumbing license. Since it does not require many parts, and the machine does most of the work, it is a high profit margin.

I therefore opened just such a business, I operated it myself shortly after completing my training program of course, and soon I was well into the profit margin. I later sold the business and then opened a new one with an even catchier name. I also periodically went to work for other similar companies to expand my knowledge in this portion of the service industry, paid training as I call it, which I feel that getting paid to learn can be better than shelling out cash to further my expertise in the more current industry standards.

After selling the second established company, I now have developed a third in the same field, which is more of a part time hobby, when the phone rings, the goal is to land the job, money in the bank. The general plan for this type of business is to set a daily goal of achieving approximately one thousand dollars per day in sales, with most of it being labor, minimal parts, and therefore it possesses a high profit margin.

Many companies have come up with different strategies or business plans relating to the service industry, I myself began by purchasing everything needed and then doing the work myself, I later evolved to selling the jobs and providing the equipment, while employees did the work. It is possible to expand by taking on a licensed partner, enabling one the ability to offer more products and services.

Employees in this field generally work on a commission based compensation plan which is to the benefit of everyone, since when they are not generating a profit they are also not costing you money. It also enables them to make a much higher income based on their particular level of experience than what they would usually make at a typical paid by the hour job.

For this type of company you can use a flat rate pricing manual so that everyone knows exactly what services are offered, what options are available, and what the cost will be up front. You can put magnetic signs on your own personal vehicle to expand your advertising potential. Your office and related staff can simply be you, with your cell phone. Now in this industry, drain cleaning machines are very expensive, as are vehicles, maintenance and fuel.

Many smart entrepreneurs today will simply hire an experienced drain cleaning technician, who has his own vehicle, drain cleaning machines, cell phone, and provides of course his own fuel for said vehicle.

The business owner simply provides the business license, liability insurance, advertising, invoices, business cards, shirts, and a flat rate pricing manual. You should also receive the phone calls and dispatch them to the service technician.

This can be a very lucrative business, even if you invested one thousand dollars to get this service up and running, you have the potential to make that amount back daily, three hundred and sixty five days per year.

The goal of the flat rate pricing manual is that the customer gets to know the price up front, before approving the work, the amount is justified because it is listed right in the book, everyone pays the same amount, with no hidden fees. Also with using the flat rate pricing guide you can make much more money, than if you were to use an hourly wage. You cannot just show up at the customers house and say, the job will take two hours and I charge five hundred dollars per hour, but knowing that most drain service calls take one or two hours to complete, and using a flat rate service manual, you can easily perform three to five calls per day, and charge anywhere from two hundred and eighty to three hundred and fifty dollars per call depending upon which drain system is clogged and what access point will be utilized to clear it with the machine.

A good, experienced service technician will achieve optimal sales which means a high profit margin for both of you. If he provides his own equipment then your maintenance fees are nonexistent. You should pay him accordingly, if he provides the hardware he is easily worth forty percent. It is a pyramid, you may begin with one employee, but you could develop a ten year plan of expanding and growing, adding one additional employee per year, so that in a ten year period of time you could be making six hundred thousand dollars per year. If you reach this point you might consider hiring a professional dispatcher. While your employees are out doing the work, perhaps you could write a book!

HANDYMAN REFERRAL SERVICE.

Here is a business, that I have direct experience with, and whom others that I personally know, have also had great success with. It is simply a referral service, it could be done with a few different topics, but the handyman service is a good one. My dining room table, laptop computer, and cell phone makes a great office space, once again you can even put magnetic signs on your personal vehicle to expand your advertising potential. You can place a free online advertisement, that you are looking to interview experienced and qualified repairmen, make sure you instruct them to bring a copy of their background check to you, check their references, ask to see pictorial portfolios of their work before entering into any business agreement. You will undoubtedly want to ensure that they are a qualified professional, with integrity, and that they also do good work. You can possibly use some of the their photos to build a web page advertising the business as well.

You provide a business license for yourself, and advertising. You are simply a referral service. The technician is an independent contractor, he or she is required to provide everything needed, including any necessary licenses or insurance, cell phone, vehicle, materials, et cetera. You can build an inexpensive website with lots of nice pictures, you place free advertisements online offering the handyman service, when the calls come in you forward the information to the independent contractor, it is his responsibility to contact the customer, set the appointment, land the job, do the work, and collect the payment. You charge twenty percent commission to the independent contractor for each completed job that you referred to him. This adds up to a good income for you, and it is fair for the contractor since he would have had to acquire advertising to obtain these jobs.

So this business required an inexpensive business license, a website costing maybe ten or twenty dollars per month, some free online advertisements, and a computer which you probably already have anyway, along with your cell phone.

When the phone rings, simply collect the potential customers contact information, the nature of the work to be done, and inform the caller that you will have your project manager contact him or her, as soon as possible.

In this situation it is usually up to the service technician to determine the cost of the job after visual inspection, or for your convenience you could simply set an hourly wage, I could suggest sixty dollars per hour for this type of work. It is advisable to have a variety of skilled technicians here, such as a licensed electrician, a licensed plumber, a concrete specialist, general laborers, landscapers, irrigation specialists. A drywall and painting crew. A glazier for window replacements, roofers, et cetera.

Always refer the correct technician for each potential job. Remember the pyramid, twenty percent commission for receiving one phone call from the customer, and dispatching a second phone call to the independent contractor, is nothing to sneeze at. You can operate a referral service while you run your drain cleaning business, sell purebred animals, and write books.

I might suggest, that once you end up with a team of qualified general laborers, it really isn't feasible to quote sixty dollars per hour apiece for them, so it may be better to quote $16 dollars per hour per laborer, and back charge each one three dollars per hour. They can be useful for digging, raking, mowing, haul away and other things.

A flat rate pricing manual really doesn't apply to a handyman referral service, but an hourly wage is normally used for this type of application.

Spend some time coming up with a catchy name for your business, and research the name to insure that it is not already in use, and that the website domain name is available.

If you have any questions or concerns in any matters, always consult a qualified attorney in advance, to make sure that any such questions are properly answered.

Always keep a positive attitude and outlook, it is just business and making money is fun, it is the American dream, the goal of business is to make money, not to spend money or to do any actual physical work.

At some points in life it seems that someone may come along who seems to be negative, I have an acquaintance who in some cases simply says, I will refer the matter to my attorney, and hangs up the phone. This seems to be very effective in her case as far as getting unruly people off of her back.

FLEA MARKET.

I myself enjoy flea markets and swap meets, I know several retired persons who make an excellent supplemental income at these functions. I have also been doing it for years, you never know what kind of collectible knick knacks and antiques that you will find at these places. On a good Saturday I have actually made anywhere from one to five hundred dollars doing this.

There are a few pointers to remember, never rent a monthly booth as this can get expensive quick and we are here to make money. Never buy merchandise mail order or online to resell, the shipping charges almost always nullify the profit margin. The best place to acquire good saleable items is the flea market itself.

Bring a wheeled cart to tote your findings in and show up early, if you don't find enough resalable items in the first day, save up for a month until you have enough, Saturdays seem to be the best day for this.

Avoid buying expensive things, the seller already wants the full market value and therefore the profit margin in those items is minimal, always haggle down to the best and lowest price, it is how it is done.

The general rule of thumb is to triple your money at the very minimum, this is the pyramid once again. However we intend to go above and beyond this amount, always quote your resale price a little bit higher than what you actually expect to receive, since potential buyers will also be trying to haggle you down, just learn to play the game.

We want to be looking for collectible knick knacks and similar things that we can purchase for one dollar, we wish to resell these things for ten dollars apiece, so when we have acquired enough items to warrant renting a cheap table for the day we will quote our resale price at twelve or fifteen dollars for this one dollar purchase that we made.

This leaves haggling room for the potential buyer which we already know they are going to do, if they offer to pay full price, fine. If not, then let them haggle you down a bit and try to get your ten dollars, I have done this many times showing a nine dollar profit for a one dollar item, it does not mean that the item is not worth the selling price, it just means that since I showed up early and have finely tuned my haggling skills, that I was able to get an

exceptionally good deal, the early bird gets the worm so to speak.
It happens to work out this way quite often, if they wish to haggle a little more it is fine, you may still get five or six dollars for that particular one dollar item, but never accept less than triple your money back.

If one buyer doesn't make a purchase, another one will be along shortly, items will sell. Learn to spot the bargains. Never pay more than one dollar apiece for popular title movies in good condition, they easily resell at three dollars apiece.

Once in a while I will purchase a ten dollar item if it is something that is popular, and I will begin by asking twenty five dollars as the resell price, not taking less than twenty after the bargaining is finished.

One key thing to look for in your purchases is the usefulness of the item, if it is something that isn't very useful, then it needs to be highly collectible or an antique, otherwise you may have difficulty reselling it.

A great place to find things is at church yard sales, they usually have great stuff at very low prices.

When you approach the flea market learn to identify the persons who are there just having a random yard sale, these are the best people to do business with, they have the best stuff at the good prices.

The regular dealers who are there every weekend already know the game, and they play it well, you would have to be really good to do profitable business with these people since they are already at expert level.

Auction houses can be a great place to make your purchases, they sometimes offer fine bargains. I once got a complete ham radio set complete with linear and microphone at one of these places for sixteen dollars, it was worth about three hundred bucks. You can usually find these places listed in the phone book, or through an online search. But remember, never ever buy a used car from them.

MINIMIZING RISK.

I would like to discuss a few things here, number one is that we should turn all aspects of our lives into a money making profitable venture, we should find a way to profit from most everything we do. We should also minimize our risks every chance we get. When I was younger I always dreamed about the flashing lights of the casinos and I entertained the notion that there must be a secret method somewhere that would enable a person to actually win money at the games instead of just being a guinea pig who goes in broke, and comes out even broker. For years I practiced playing different realistic casino video games at home, trying different strategies.

Then one day it dawned on me, there is in fact just such a way, first of all, I had been looking at the wrong games.

The biggest house advantage is that they are expert at each game, they are hoping that you are inexperienced, they will be happy to teach you of course, the hard way, at the cost of losing your money. No system is foolproof, but instead we wish to maximize our odds of winning. This is something I have done many times while on vacation.

I have actually won thousands of dollars at casinos in Las Vegas. I like to go on yearly road trips to sight see different portions of America, along the way I will visit casinos to have a little fun and generate some extra cash.

The game I discovered how to win at is roulette. It is a very simple game, at first glance I figured it must be very hard to win if you pick a number when there are so many the ball could land on.

Wrong answer baby!, roulette is the game of winners in my book, it is time to ring in the new year by raking in piles of glorious cash. I like a big casino with lots of roulette tables, I can hop skip and jump around from one table to the other. I will mix in a little black jack as well, and some slots. On the slot machines I like wheel of fortune and progressive jackpots. Always play the max bet, and play the game three times. If it didn't hit a jackpot, move to a different machine. I have used this technique many times to find the machine that is ready to pay out a jackpot.

Now with blackjack, I recommend playing conservatively, that is to say we want to avoid busting, leave that to the dealer, he will do it. I like to start with the minimum bet, each time I lose I will triple my bet, when the dealer busts, I just made a profit and now I start over again at the minimum bet.

Sometimes you will notice that the dealer will hit streaks of busting, one hand right after the other. This is when I start betting big. As soon as I notice the dealer has busted twice in a row, I will start betting the maximum bet, just let him bust a few times and we will collect our winnings. I begin my blackjack game with a buy in of anywhere from one hundred, to two hundred dollars. I relax, and settle into the game just piddling along with my tripling strategy, if I wish to be more conservative I will reduce my betting system to a doubling strategy. I am just waiting for the right time to make my move and pounce.

When the dealer begins his pattern losing streak of busting, I start betting the maximum bet for a few hands only, we don't want to push too far here, because eventually he will begin winning again.

So I begin with anywhere from one to two hundred dollars, when my pile of chips increases to eight or nine hundred dollars I quit and walk away, cold turkey, no matter what. You have to know when to walk away, if you don't you might end up handing all of that money back to the casino, and this we do not want to do. I want to throw all the cash on the bed and roll around in it, yippee I am a winner!

Don't forget, the first thing you want to do when you enter a casino is to join the players club, get the club card, ask for an extra card as well. We can rack up free meals, free betting chips, gifts, and discounted rooms while we make money, and have fun. If the casino is offering free drinks, stick to the nonalcoholic beverages. The casino would just love to loosen you up a little and get you rolling on a nice, long, losing streak, and that's why they offer you the free drinks. So choose wisely, grapefruit juice anyone? Oops, I seem to have left my extra club card in a popular slot machine and walked away, now someone else is inadvertently playing the machine while racking up free meals and prizes for me on my players club account, I wish I could remember to stop leaving my card laying around in the machines like that, I will just have to wait until that person is finished utilizing the game, so that I can retrieve my card.

And now it is time for dessert, let us journey over to the roulette tables, we are about to astonish the dealer, as he steadily runs out of chips due to our winnings.

ROULETTE.

Now I do not know if other persons have figured out this strategy or not. My personal roulette technique is something that I came up with on my own. I have spent hundreds of hours playing roulette, practicing and honing my skills. I like to warm up and keep my techniques in shape by regularly playing at home, especially before I go to the real casino.

In roulette there are many bets that you can place, some of them are known as inside bets, and some of them are known as outside bets. I will not need to cover all of the possible bets which can be placed, but instead I will focus on the ones that I prefer, which I believe have a much better chance of winning. No strategy is foolproof, it only serves to increase your odds of winning, while reducing your chances of losing, at the same time.

If you play three hands and lose every one of them, I recommend moving to a different table, I prefer a busy table and I buy in at one hundred dollars worth of five dollar chips. Definitely if you have lost five hands in a row, it is time to move elsewhere. The key to each game is to find the one which is ready to pay out a short winning streak, play a few hands, collect the payout, and move on. I usually don't stay at one roulette table more than thirty minutes.

I like the outside bets. They pay out at two to one. There are two groups of three outside bets. The first one is right in front of you, it consists of the first dozen numbers which are one through twelve.

The second dozen consists of the numbers thirteen through twenty four, and the third dozen consists of the numbers twenty five through thirty six. This is my favorite bet, I will begin by placing two equal bets of fifteen dollars each, the first outside bet I place on the second dozen, the second bet I place on the third dozen. I am now covering close to two thirds of the roulette board, in two bets. This gives me a much higher chance of winning than if I were to bet on a single number. I am covering all numbers from thirteen to thirty six, if one of these two bets wins, I will profit fifteen dollars, even though one of those bets was lost. So I put up thirty dollars, I believe I have great than a sixty percent chance of winning, and when I win I now have forty five dollars. If I lose a hand I will triple my bet until I win, once I win I will go back to betting groups of fifteen dollars again.

Now, as with other games, sometimes the table is hot and you will hit a winning streak. When this occurs I increase my two bets to the maximum amount that the table will allow. At this point I only play a few hands. Once I have nine hundred dollars in front of me I quit, I walk away cold turkey, no matter what. That does not mean that I will not go to another game and resume play, because I very well may, but it does mean that since I started with one hundred dollars, I showed a profit of eight hundred bucks. I will put that eight hundred bucks into an interest bearing savings account, and I will use the remaining Benjamin franklin, for dinner, fuel, and or to resume play at a new game.

I don't always stay at the table all the way up to the nine hundred dollar mark, although I did actually stay at one roulette table until I had won close to three thousand dollars once, but that is where I learned that you must set a point to walk away, because eventually there comes a point when you hit a losing streak, and losing money is not what we are about.

I generally will set my winning goal to be three hundred dollars, which means a two hundred dollar profit. Once I am up to three hundred dollars, I will walk away and take a break, pocketing my two hundred dollar win. Unless I see that the table is in a hot winning streak, then I will start betting the maximum bet for anywhere from three to five hands, and then I am finished for the moment. We want to leave the table with a final win if we can, not the last hand played being a loss.

If I really just want to sit there and play for a longer period of time, just for the fun of it, then I will reduce my bets to five dollars apiece, increasing to ten or fifteen dollars per bet during winning streaks. Piddling along with two five dollar bets I can play for a long time, waiting for the right moment to pounce, and clean house. This technique is very simple and easy so that anyone can do it, it is simply a very smart way to bet.

The second group of three outside bets are at the right end of the roulette table, the first column which begins with the number one and ends with the number thirty four.

The second column which begins with the number two, and ends with the number thirty five.

The third column which begins with the number three, and ends with the number thirty six.

These three columns also pay out at two to one odds. The same strategy can be used here, that we used before. Simply pick two of the columns and place equal bets in each of them, once again you are covering most of the board, therefore you have increased your chance of winning. If you placed two equal bets of ten dollars each on two of these columns, and if one of those two bets wins, you will now have thirty dollars, which is a profit of ten dollars. I can play several rounds per hour so it can add up to a considerable hourly wage just piddling along at the roulette table making ten and fifteen dollar bets. I usually choose to place my bets in the second dozen column, and the third dozen column, this is where I have had the greatest amount of success. Remember, three losses in a row, we walk away. You also do not have to do the doubling and tripling strategy, but I personally use it and I have had great success with it. During winning streaks I will randomly throw down bets of fifty dollars or more, winning a good little pile of chips which I will put in my pocket, and then immediately go back to placing five dollar bets.

Don't forget, if you win in the hundreds, it is fine to spend some of the money, but be conservative and put the larger portion of it into a savings plan with interest.

Choose the games that you like, and practice them at home on a realistic video game system, one that closely imitates casino games. Practice makes perfect. We want to become a master of our chosen game. The skill level of the dealer needs to pale in comparison to our own.

HOW TO MAKE MONEY.

STAYING OUT OF DEBT.

One thing that I firmly believe in, is to never ever, borrow money. This only puts you further in debt, especially if the loan will accrue interest or requires collateral. Being broke is not improved by putting your home or vehicle at risk of forfeiture, or by racking up more debt with unreasonable high interest rates on top of it.

This also applies to buying a vehicle from a dealership, either new or used. Do not finance your vehicle, this adds tons of interest to the loan and I feel it is a crooked scam. Car dealers are sometimes not known for having integrity or even knowing the meaning of the word. I have some advice for you from my own personal experience about buying a vehicle.

First of all, save your money until you have enough to pay cash outright for the total cost of your purchase. Second, never buy a vehicle from an auction unless you are planning on using that vehicle as a yard ornament or as a sign showing people what not to buy.

Third, when you step onto the car lot ignore the salesman, do not answer any of his questions or give him any type of information, just pretend that he does not exist, if he is harassing you ask him to give you some space, and that you will approach him when you are ready. Now the first thing we want to do now is to examine all of the vehicles on the lot to determine if they actually have one that you want, if they do have the automobile for you, approach the salesmen, tell him you want the total cost of this vehicle in writing, the full sales price. Once again, do not answer any of his questions or give him any information, simply demand the full price in writing, once you have it you can begin haggling, offer less money, don't answer any questions because anything you say they will use against you in their blatant assault upon your poor wallet. Haggle like you mean it, when it is all said and done, just tell them the price is ridiculous and that you will shop elsewhere, by this time there is only one piece of information that they asked you for that was acceptable to give them, and that is your cell phone number. The game of haggling changes once they see their potential customer is leaving, and appears to be interested in shopping with a competitor. Drive away from the dealership, it will not be long before they call you wanting you to come back, they will now be willing to haggle a little bit more. If you come to an agreement, make sure that the salesman draws up a contract, which specifically lists every minor detail of the agreement, make him put each and every one of his promises in writing, especially if you notice that he paints his hair with what appears to be shoe polish.

Now once everything is locked down in writing, you can inform him that you will write a check for the full amount so there will be no need to apply any interest or finance charges. Also, they will want to try and get your trade in vehicle from you, at your loss of course. I recommend not allowing them to even discuss it with you, if they ask you about your current vehicle, just ignore this and respond by asking a question of your own. Either keep it as an extra vehicle, or sell it on your own to a private citizen, and not to a dealership.

I hope that you profit from my advice, live long and prosper. S.A.S. 2013.

OTHER BOOKS BY STEVEN SCHOOL.

Alchemy and the green lion.
Alchemy and the Golden Water.
Alchemy and the Peacocks Tail.
Grandmas Delicious Recipes.
Karate Secrets Revealed.
Trophy Wife.

www.ingramcontent.com/pod-product-compliance
Lightning Source LLC
Chambersburg PA
CBHW051422170526
45165CB00004BA/1928